I0476063

Make-Money-Online Series

How to Start Your Online Photography Store

Step-by-Step Guide to Selling Your Photos Online

Blake Webster

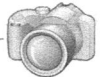

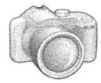

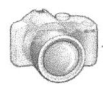
Books by Blake Webster

Greener Living Today: Forty Ways to a Greener Lifestyle

How to Start Your Online Affiliate Store: Step-by-Step Guide to Making Money Online

Environmentalists in Action: Profiles of Green Pioneers

How to Self-Publish Your Book the CreateSpace Way

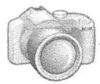
Introduction

The first camera I remember taking photos with was my parents' Kodak Instamatic in the late sixties. They eventually gave me the camera and I continued using it until 1973, when I met my wife, Elaine. She owned a Polaroid, and we used that until 1981, when we purchased a Russian 35mm camera. It was a good starter camera for learning how to shoot 35mm, but all the labels were in Russian. It was also heavy and cumbersome, so the following year we traded it in for a Nikon 35mm point and shoot.

In 1996, I became a web and multimedia developer and started designing templates for Dreamweaver and FrontPage. In 2003, aiming to step up the quality of my designs, I added photography, yet another element to enhance the look of my sites and, I hoped, my sales. I couldn't afford to pay the expensive royalties commanded by the large stock photo companies, so I started taking my own pictures.

I upgraded to a newer 35mm camera, the Nikon N75. In that year, 2003, digital cameras were just coming out and still very expensive. Moreover, digital quality and mega pixels were still quite low.

 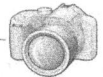

As I took photos for my design templates, I soon developed a renewed interest in photography, a great way to express one's creativity. I've long been drawn to architectural themes, so taking photos of buildings was a perfect way to enhance my online business designs. I started developing Flash photo galleries that would allow other photographers to display their portfolios using a professional and intuitive interface.

As I continued taking photos, it became clear I had to find an alternative to the high cost of developing my work. So I went out and bought one of the first high-end digital cameras, the Nikon Coolpix 8700. Now I was able to take as many photos as I wanted and have them web-ready instantly.

That's when I decided to set up my first online photography store. Soon I was shooting and processing high-resolution photos and selling them online.

Shooting high-quality photographs often depends on being in the right place at the right time. Beyond that, though, elements such as composition and lighting need to be mastered. As my passion for photography grew, my skills improved.

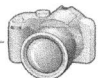

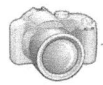
Then I decided to expand the sale of my photos beyond my online store, to take my template designs to the next step, using higher-end imagery.

One of my clients, a professional photographer in Florida, was selling his Nikon D200 digital camera, complete with wide-angle lens. I bought the camera and still use it today. Given how it improved the quality of my work, it was one of the best investments I've ever made.

As I created new images, I added them to my online catalog and also sold them through other stock-photography sites, such as iStockphoto and fotolia.

I usually divide photographers into three categories: amateur photographers, photographers and professional photographers. Amateurs take photos for family and fun, with no commercial motivation. Photographers have a special passion for photography and might sell some of their photos. Professionals hire out their services and sell their images.

In this book I aim to help you advance from amateur photographer to one of the other two categories.

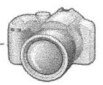

This is a guide to setting up an online store for selling your photography. Even if you are a professional, you may lack the budget for hiring developers to establish your online presence, and may lack the time to do it yourself.

I will offer three approaches in different price ranges. Two of the recommended software applications will make use of the WordPress content-management system. The third is a stand-alone software application that requires a MySql database. It has all the store features built in and makes use of various css design templates to enhance the look and feel of your store.

We will focus on just three approaches because I believe they are the most cost-effective and user-friendly ways to start an online photography store.

 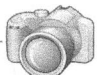

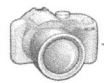

Table of Contents

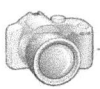

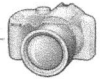

Why Run an Online Photography Store?

If you're a photographer, why not look for ways to promote and sell your digital work?

Website developers, online publications, advertisers, and others are always on the lookout for stock photography. Often they buy from higher-end suppliers, such as iStock Photos and Fotolia. These photos can be costly in order to compensate the photographers who have signed on through partner programs. Partner programs allow photographers to create an account and sell their work on commission.

You can always apply to these companies and try selling your photos through their outlets, but chances are, unless the quality of your images is extraordinary, you will become lost in the crowd.

That's why you should consider starting your own online photography store. By promoting the site and profiling your own work, you can set a fair price for your photos and eliminate the commission structure.

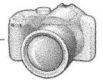

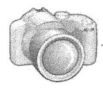

If you are an event photographer, or for that matter a photographer who simply believes his work is worth selling, running your own online store allows you to market your photos and prints online, expanding your potential audience and making it more convenient for your customers.

One issue I had with some high-end suppliers was their strict policy on quality, which can be highly subjective. Admittedly, though, they are looking for very-high-end photography. Another time I had a stock-photo company reject some of my photos, not because of the quality, but because they didn't believe photos in the "vintage car" category would sell well in their catalog. So I took those photos, uploaded them into my storefront, and couldn't believe how well they sold.

Recommended Software for Photography Storefronts

In this section I will discuss both the software application that I use for my online photography store and two other options that, though more affordable, still deliver a similar capacity to sell digital products.

PhotoStore

PhotoStore allows you to set up a complete photo-selling website on your server or hosting space. In minutes, you can start selling photos on your website. There are no monthly fees and no commission fees.

PhotoStore is ideal for event photographers wanting to sell images or prints to their customers online. It also works for anyone who wants to sell stock photos online.

With PhotoStore:

- You can sell photos, vector art, zip files, and videos.
- You can sell various sizes of the same photo or video.
- You can sell prints, artwork, products, and more.
- Customers can instantly download after payment.

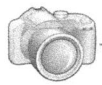

PhotoStore Features:

- Built-in shopping cart and ecommerce system to accept credit cards and/or check payments.
- Email notifications to both you and the customer upon purchase.
- Connects to any of the following payment gateways: PayPal, 2Checkout.com, Authorize.net, Plug n' Pay, MyGate.co.za. Others can be added.

The program sells for $249. You can purchase PhotoStore at the following address:

http://ktools.net/photostore/

PhotoStore is the program I use for my photography site, MediaStockPhotos:

http://www.mediastockphotos.com

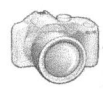

ShopperPress

ShopperPress is a WordPress shopping cart that works with any standard Wordpress 2.8+ installation.

ShopperPress is a turn-key ready "out of the box" shopping-cart solution. You simply install, select your template, add products, and you're ready to start accepting orders. It takes minutes from download to install, and it's easy to set up and manage.

ShopperPress includes over 20 quality shopping-cart theme designs and lots of great features, such as shipping options, tax options, coupon codes, articles, promotions, payment gateways, and more.

ShopperPress combines the security, stability, and flexibility of Wordpress with the features and designs of an ecommerce storefront to create the most popular shopping-cart themes for Wordpress. Themes include Mobile Phone Shopper, Kitchen Shopper, Bridal Shopper, Software shopper, and more.

ShopperPress sells for $79. You can purchase it at the following address:

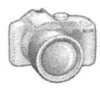

http://www.shopperpress.com

You can view my sample site, Media Design Photography, at the following address:

http://www.mediadesignphotography.com/

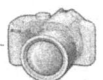

WordPress eStore Plugin

This sleek WordPress shopping-cart plugin allows you to sell any form of digital products and services from your wordpress blog, and to do it securely with complete automation. Once you set it up, the whole process works on its own, including buying and delivering the product without revealing the real URL of the product.

Features include:

- Security of digital assets.
- Easy checkout.
- Ease of use and design.
- Autoresponder integration.
- NextGen gallery integration.
- WP eMember integration.
- Affiliate software integration.
- Lightweight shopping cart.
- PayPal integration.

WordPress eStore Plugin sells for $39.95. Learn more about it at the following address:

http://www.tipsandtricks-hq.com/

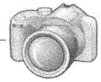

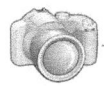

Click on the eStore image in the right column under Tips and Tricks Hot Items.

You can view my sample site, Media Design Photography, at the following address:

http://www.mediadesignphotos.com

Getting Started

Choose and Register a Domain Name

The first step is to register a domain name. I recommend choosing a domain name that contains keywords pertaining to photography or the name of your business.

Examples:

www.mediastockphotos.com
www.mediadesignphotos.com
www.mediadesignphotography.com

I register all of my domains with GoDaddy, one of the largest registrars, but you can use any registrar you feel comfortable with, such as HostGator or Network Solutions.

I usually start by conducting a domain search for my best ideas. If a domain name I like is available, I head over to Google and do a search on www.thenameofthedomain.com to see if it's recently been in use.

 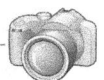

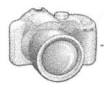

If it doesn't turn up, I do the same search without the www. If it still doesn't produce any results, I repeat the process at Yahoo. If I come up empty there, I'll usually go ahead and register the domain.

I do all this to find out if the domain has recently been in use and, if so, what kind of site was it? Was it legitimate or "spammy"? I also try to determine if the domain has been de-indexed from Google for some reason. If you come up with a name you love and it's available, conduct a search on sites such as Just Dropped.com, www.justdropped.com. This will provide you with a complete breakdown of the domain's history.

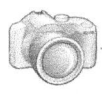

Find a Hosting Provider

Once you've registered your domain, you need to set it up with a hosting provider. If you have a GoDaddy account, you can use GoDaddy as the provider.

I prefer to use hosting companies that provide cPanel, which is a control panel for the back-end administration of my domains and sites. GoDaddy is fine, but it can be a little slow and cumbersome when it comes to setting up email accounts and MySql databases, a relational data-base-management system.

After years of running dedicated servers and using a multitude of hosting companies, I finally decided on HostGator. A large provider out of Texas, HostGator offers top-notch support, good backup, and a server system that responds quickly to setup procedures.

After choosing your provider, you must change the name server information so that the domain points to your new hosting service. If you are using hosting from the same company with which you registered the domain, you probably won't have to change this. Check with the hosting company's technical support.

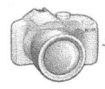

Name server information will look something like this:

NS1.1111.HOSTGATOR.COM and
NS2.1112.HOSTGATOR.COM

After setting up a hosting account, you will usually be provided with the name server information by email, along with setup instructions.

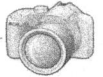

Download a FTP Program

Suggested FTP Programs

FTP stands for file transfer protocol and is the method used to copy a file from one host to another over a TCP/IP-based network, such as the Internet.

Applications were originally interactive command-line tools with a standardized command syntax, but graphical user interfaces have been developed for all desktop operating systems in use today.

When I first started moving files from my local computer to the server in 1995, you had to have a command of the Unix language, for which there was no technical support. Today the interfaces are easy to understand and user friendly.

Some of the more popular ftp programs include WS FTP, Cute FTP, FileZilla, Smart FTP, Go FTP, and WinSCP.

As a user of WS FTP since 1996, I like its user-friendly interface. It can serve as a local file manager when you're not using it for transferring files. It also streamlines tasks such as renaming remote files and changing their file permissions.

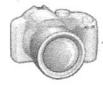

WS FTP Pro sells for $54.95 with no support, or $89.95 with one year's support.

Learn more at the following address:

http://www.ipswitchft.com/Products/Ws_Ftp_Pro/

If you're looking for a free ftp program, I recommend WinSCP.

WinSCP is an open-source SFTP client and FTP client for Windows. Its main function is to facilitate secure file transfers between a local and a remote computer. Beyond this, WinSCP offers basic file-manager functionality. It uses Secure Shell (SSH) for those who prefer to have root access abilities. Having root access to the server gives you the ability to take full control of that server.

Learn more at the following address:

http://winscp.net/eng/index.php

Set Up a MySql Database

cPanel

You can create a new MySql database by selecting MySql Databases from the Databases section of cPanel. Assign the database a name that corresponds with the name of your domain. If, for example, your site is about pets and the domain name is www.mypets.com, you could give a database the name "mypets."

Next, create a user for the database. In the Databases section, select MySql Databases, then scroll down to the section called MySql Users. Create a username that also corresponds with the name of the domain, then assign a password. Click the Create User button.

Now you need to add the new user to the new database. Scroll down the same section to the area labeled Add User to Database. From the User dropdown options, select your new user. From the Database dropdown options, select your new database. Click the Add button.

In the next window, select Enable All Privileges and click on the Make Changes button.

 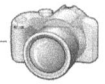

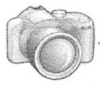

That's it! Your database is all set up.

Screenshot #1

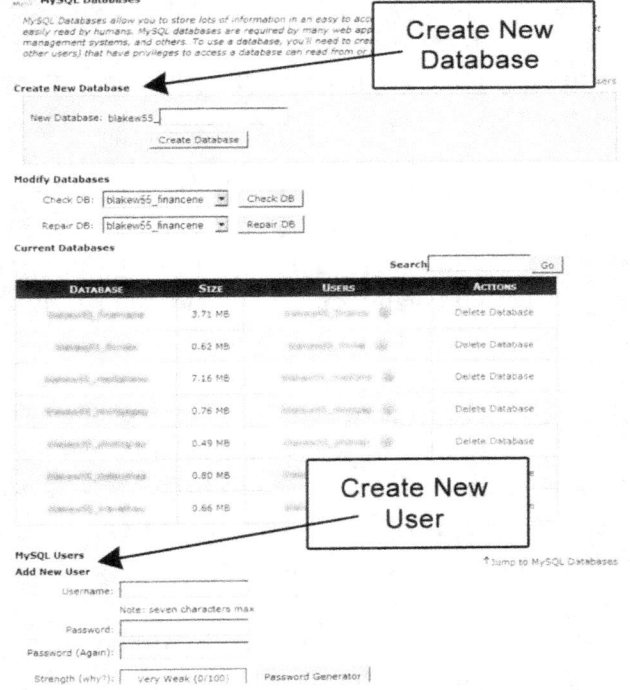

Screenshot #2

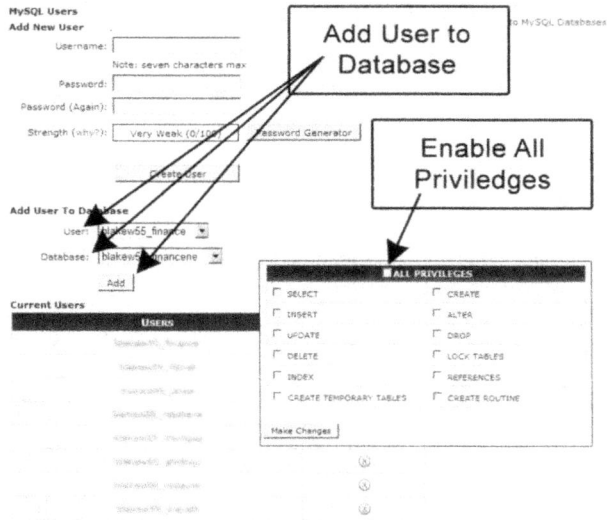

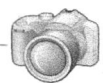

GoDaddy

Go Daddy is an Internet domain registrar and web-hosting company that also sells e-business-related software and services.

▪ Log into your GoDaddy account, then select Hosting from the left-column navigation menu.

▪ Open your hosting account by clicking on the Launch button.

▪ From the top menu bar, select Databases/MySql.

▪ Click on the Create Database button.

▪ Enter the database description, name, and password.

▪ Select the MySql version. Version 5.0 is fine unless your software instructions indicate otherwise.

▪ Click OK. You will see that the setup is pending; it could take as long as a half hour to complete.

 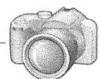

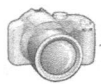

After setup is completed, you can click on the Edit button for your new database; find out the local path in order to edit the WordPress configuration file.

Screenshot #3

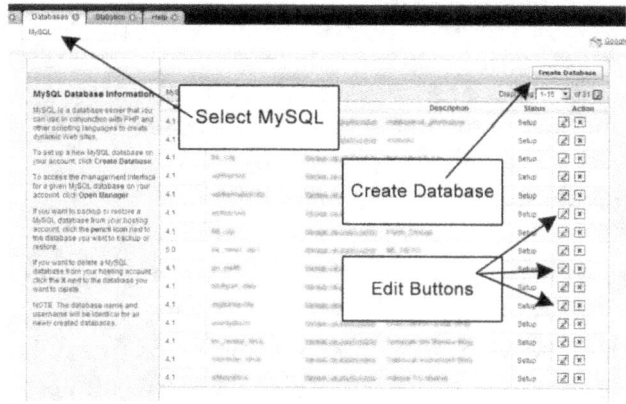

Screenshot #4

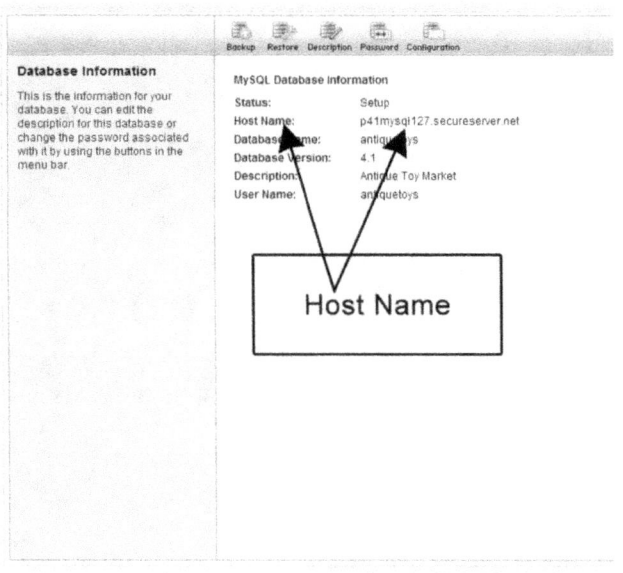

 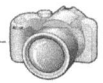

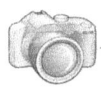

Wordpress

Wordpress is the setup choice for two of the storefront options in this book. WordPress is the content-management system used by most websites, and it's particularly valuable for your online store. The software recommendations I offer later all require WordPress.

An open-source blog-publishing platform powered by PHP and MySQL, WordPress can be used for basic content management. It includes many features, including a user-friendly administration panel, a rich plugin architecture, and an advanced templating system.

I will address only the overall setup for Wordpress using cPanel. The process is basically the same with all providers, though some have slightly different methods of setup.

Step One

Go to cPanel, and add your domain to your account by selecting Add-on Domains from the Domains section.

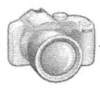
Step Two

Create a new MySql database, as described in the previous chapter.

Step Three

Download the latest release of WordPress. Since it's open source, you can download the files for free.

Go to the WordPress homepage, www.wordpress.org, and click on the button labeled Download WordPress (Version Number). Save the files to your hard drive. The version changes on a regular basis. I suggest downloading the most recent version, though previous versions are also available.

 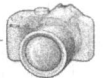

Installing WordPress

To install WordPress:

1. Unzip the files. You should see everything you need to upload inside of a folder labeled wordpress.
2. Open the PHP file labeled, usually, wp-config.php. It may be labeled wp-config-sample.php; if so, rename it wp-config.php. This is the file that allows us to define the database settings.
3. Open the PHP file in a text editor such as Notepad.
4. Look for the following lines near the top of the file and edit them accordingly, inserting the database name, user name, and password you chose when setting up the database:

define('DB_NAME', 'your_cpanel_database_name')

define('DB_USER', 'your_cpanel_user_name')

define('DB_PASSWORD', 'your_cpanel_password')

5. Save the file and upload all files into the root directory of your new website.

 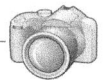

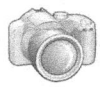

6. After the upload is complete, call up the new domain in your web browser and follow the instructions. Installation should take about two seconds.

7. Log into the Dashboard using the assigned login information.

8. Select Users in the left column, then change the password to something you can remember.

WordPress is now installed and ready for modifications.

 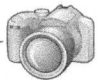

Install WordPress with Fantistico

Fantastico is a commercial script library that automates the installation of web applications to a website. Fantastico scripts are executed from the administration area of a website control panel such as cPanel. According to its website, Fantastico is installed on ten thousand servers, with a million users worldwide.

I find Fantastico fast and easy to use, but I encountered problems with some of my setups in relation to certain WordPress applications. I prefer to set up WordPress using standard installation methods, which involve creating a database, configuring and uploading the most recent version of WordPress.

To install WordPress and a MySql database using Fantastico within cPanel, go to the bottom of your cPanel admin interface to a section titled Software/Services.

Click on Fantistico DeLux. Follow the instructions and Fantastico will set up the MySql database and install the latest version of WordPress.

 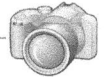

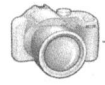

General WordPress Setup

Settings

The first thing I do is add keywords to my tagline.

- In the left column, under Settings, select General.

- In the second field, labeled Tagline, enter your most important keywords separated by commas. These words will appear in your title tags and help your search-engine positioning. One quick way to search for keywords is to use the keyword tool that Google provides (www.google.com/sktool).

The Search-based Keyword Tool generates keyword ideas specific to your website. The tool helps you identify advertising opportunities that aren't currently being used in your AdWords ad campaigns. It also tailors keywords and other data (such as the amount of competition for the keyword, the suggested bid, and more) based on your language or country/territory settings.

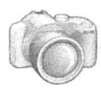

Based on your URLs, the Search-based Keyword Tool displays a list of relevant user queries that have occurred on Google with some frequency over the past year. The keywords are organized by category. Click any category to expand and view its subcategories. If applicable, you'll also see the keywords organized by brand names.

Permalinks

The next-to-last step in the setup process is to adjust your permalink settings.

- In the left column, under Settings, select Permalinks.

- Enable Custom Structure and add the following in the field to the right: /%postname%/

- This will assign permanent URLs to your individual weblog posts, thus making them more search-engine friendly.

Plugins

Plugins can extend WordPress, making it do almost anything you can imagine, such as adding contact forms, photo galleries, online stores, and more.

To activate the plugins, a) select Plugins in the left column of the Dashboard, b) choose the plugin to be activated, and c) click on the link labeled Activate.

In general, follow each plugin's instructions for installation. All will require that you upload the files to the plugin folder of WordPress.

I recommend the following plugins for basic setup.

Google XML Sitemaps

This plugin will generate a sitemaps.org-compatible sitemap of your WordPress blog, which is supported by Ask.com, Google, MSN Search, and YAHOO.

You can download it at this address:

http://www.arnebrachhold.de/projects/wordpress-plugins

 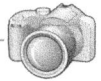

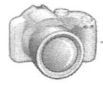
Robots Meta

This plugin allows you to a) add all the appropriate robots meta tags to your pages and feeds, b) disable unused archives, and 3) nofollow unnecessary links.

Download it at the following address:

http://yoast.com/wordpress/meta-robots-wordpress-plugin

RSS Footer

This allows you to add a line of content to the end of your RSS feed articles.

Find it at the following address:

http://yoast.com/wordpress/rss-footer

WP-SpamFree

This is an extremely powerful anti-spam plugin that virtually eliminates comment spam.

At last, you can enjoy a spam-free WordPress blog! It also includes a spam-free contact form captcha feature. Captcha is a type of challenge-response test used to ensure that a response is not computer-generated.

You can download it here:

http://www.hybrid6.com/webgeek/plugins/wp-spamfree

 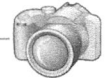

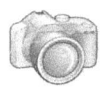
General Setup Instructions

What follows is a brief overview and quick-start guide to the setup involved for each of the three programs I am profiling: PhotoStore, ShpperPress, and WordPress eStore Plugin.

Regardless of your technical skills, setup for these stores is not difficult.

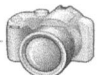

PhotoStore

If you are serious about selling your photos online, PhotoStore is one of the best solutions available, as you will discover after comparing the setup procedures for each recommended store application.

Installing PhotoStore

PhotoStore requires a MySql database.

After setting up your new database, per the instructions provided earlier, you will need to import the file database.sql—located in the "assets/database" folder—into your new database. You can use phpMyAdmin to do this if your host has it installed.

If you are not sure where to set up or import a database, contact your hosting provider. For help using phpMyAdmin, visit http://www.phpmyadmin.net.

Next, open the file database.php located in the "website" folder and enter your database username, password, database name, and database host (in most cases the database host will be "localhost" for the new database). Save the file.

 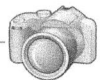

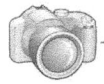
Using your FTP program, upload all files in the "website" folder to your server.

Once your files are uploaded to your server, CHMOD the "ftp," "gal images," "logo," "sample_videos," "stock_photos," "stock_videos," "temp," "uploaded_files," and "uploaded_images" folders to 777.

Screenshot #5

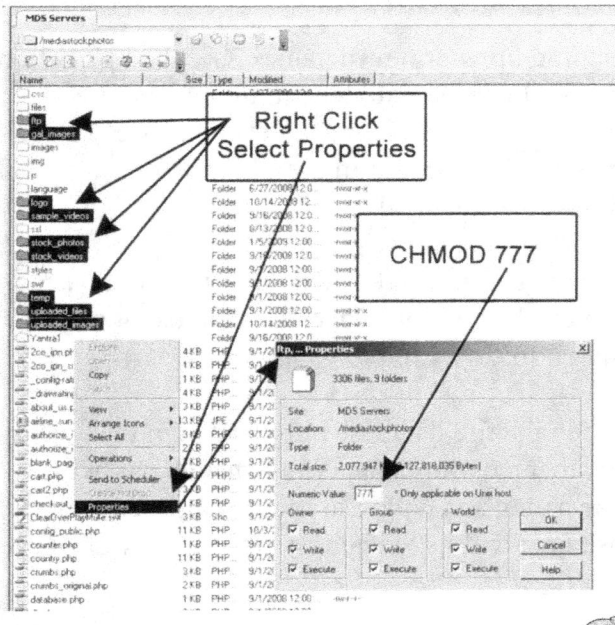

CHMOD the file "tree_items.js" to 666 located in the "js" directory.

CHMOD the folder "data" located in the "manager" directory to 777.

Now go to http://yourdomain.com/manager (or http://yourdomain.com/photostore_dir/manager if you have PhotoStore uploaded in a subdirectory of your hosting) and enter your product code. Your product code was sent to you in an email when you purchased PhotoStore. If you do not know your product code, contact Ktools.net support at http://www.ktools.net/contact.php.

You should now be able to log in using the following information:

username: admin
password: admin

Finally, you should configure the settings of your new store. Select Settings in the left navigation column. From here you can define essential site settings, such as the name of your store, tag lines, email address, keywords, and meta tag description for SEO purposes.

Your site is set up and ready to go.

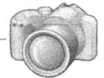

Using PhotoStore

PhotoStore is one of the most sophisticated programs on the market. Once inside the Main Site Settings area, you can define every aspect of the look and function of your new store.

Here's a brief overview of each section.

Site

Here you can define the name of your site, select a design style, and set up your Featured photo section, payment options, and subscription options.

Display

This section defines the settings for the number of photos per page, newest photos, featured photos, popular photos, and photo search results.

You can also adjust the settings for thumbnail sizes, water-marking, large image preview sizes, and language.

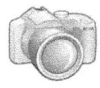

Menu

Here you find the settings for the left navigation menu of your store. You can choose between a classic menu or a collapsible menu. You can also define the mouseover hover view size of your thumbnail displays.

Sell

These settings control the stores selling capacity. You can disable or enable your ability to sell prints/products and digital downloads. You can also define a default price per photo if no price is entered when adding a new photo.

Orders

These settings are used to control order options. If you want customers to be able to download immediately after paying online with a credit card, make sure to check the option to "force approve" all orders. This section also allows you to define the number of days that a customer account remains active—that is, how many days they have to download after you charge their account.

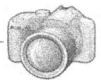

Screenshot #6

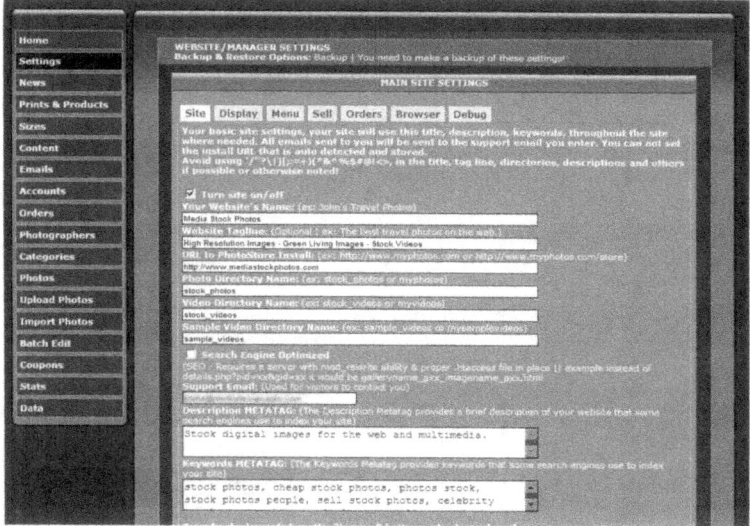

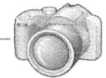

Adding New Photos

When you want to add new photos, PhotoStore makes it easy.

First, you need to create your categories. Select Categories from the left menu. Click on the New button, add your category title, and click Save.

PhotoStore allows you to resize thumbnail images, thumbnail previews, and large previews. PhotoStore will also create different resolution sizes for sale, if you enable those features when adding a new photo.

Make sure your photos are saved at a high resolution of 300 DPI, which is print quality.

To add a new photo:

- Select Photos from the left menu.
- Select a category from the Category drop-down menu.

 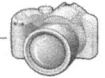

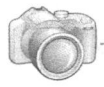
- Click the New button. Here you will add the title, searchable keywords, product description, subcategory (if any), and indicate if the product is featured, active, and if you want make the digital version available for sale. You can also decide whether to allow all image sizes to be sold.
- Upload the image from your local computer. You can only upload .jpg files.
- Define the price.
- Define the image quality, usually 300 DPI.
- Set pricing for other photo sizes. PhotoStore will automatically create a Large version (800 pixels), Medium version (600 pixels), and Small version (400 pixels).
- Click on the Save button. PhotoStore goes to work making the conversions and setting the images up for download after purchase.
- Your photo is now ready for purchase.

Screenshot #7

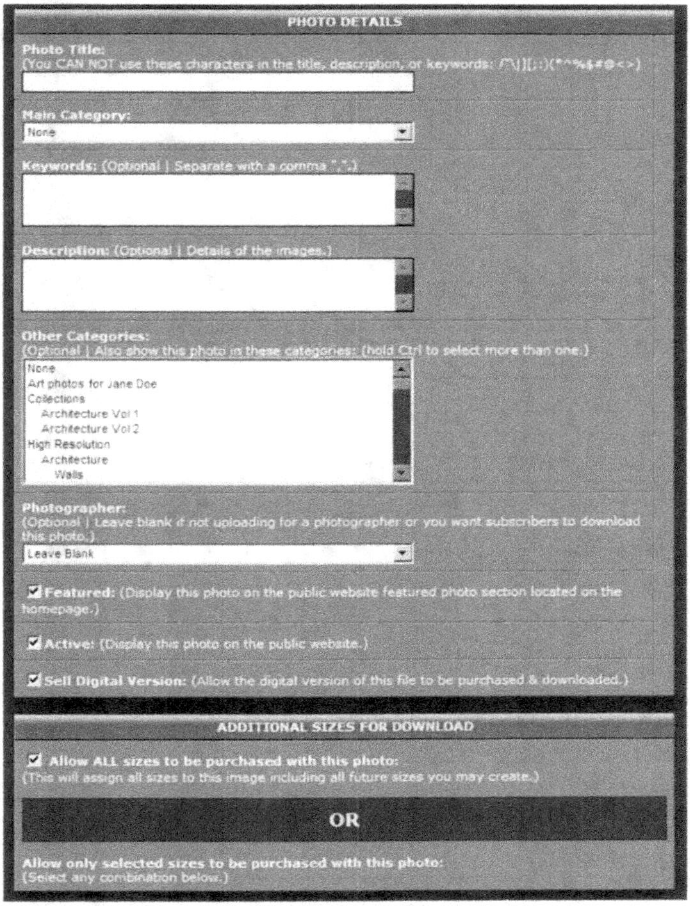

Screenshot #8

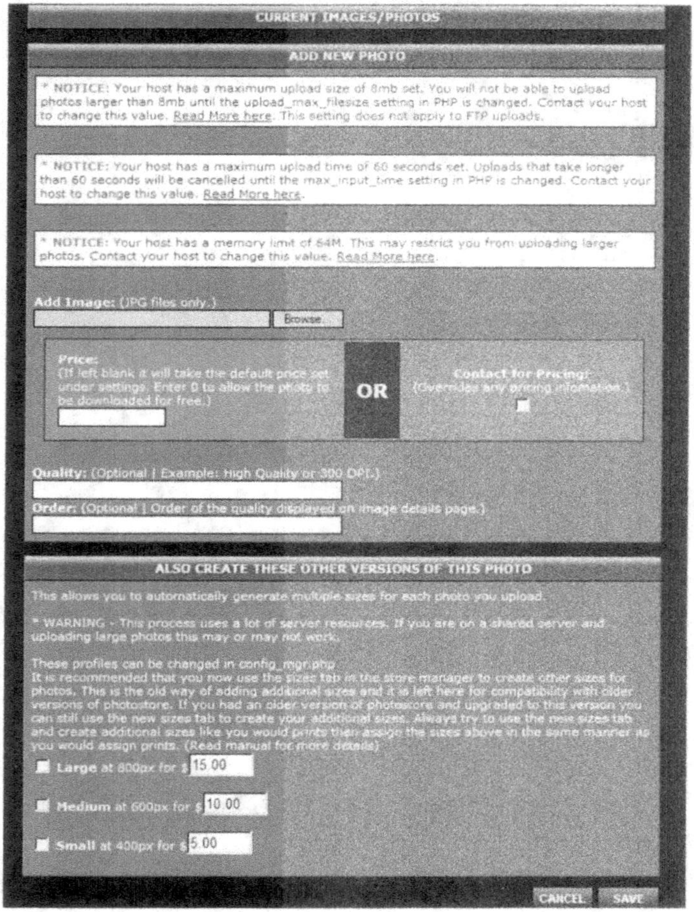

CURRENT IMAGES/PHOTOS

ADD NEW PHOTO

* NOTICE: Your host has a maximum upload size of 8mb set. You will not be able to upload photos larger than 8mb until the upload_max_filesize setting in PHP is changed. Contact your host to change this value. Read More here. This setting does not apply to FTP uploads.

* NOTICE: Your host has a maximum upload time of 60 seconds set. Uploads that take longer than 60 seconds will be cancelled until the max_input_time setting in PHP is changed. Contact your host to change this value. Read More here.

* NOTICE: Your host has a memory limit of 64M. This may restrict you from uploading larger photos. Contact your host to change this value. Read More here.

Add Image: (JPG files only.)
[   ] Browse...

Price:
(If left blank it will take the default price set under settings. Enter 0 to allow the photo to be downloaded for free.)
[   ]

OR

Contact for Pricing:
(Overrides any pricing information.)
[ ]

Quality: (Optional | Example: High Quality or 300 DPI.)

Order: (Optional | Order of the quality displayed on image details page.)

ALSO CREATE THESE OTHER VERSIONS OF THIS PHOTO

This allows you to automatically generate multiple sizes for each photo you upload.

* WARNING - This process uses a lot of server resources. If you are on a shared server and uploading large photos this may or may not work.

These profiles can be changed in config_mgr.php
It is recommended that you now use the sizes tab in the store manager to create other sizes for photos. This is the old way of adding additional sizes and it is left here for compatibility with older versions of photostore. If you had an older version of photostore and upgraded to this version you can still use the new sizes tab to create your additional sizes. Always try to use the new sizes tab and create additional sizes like you would prints then assign the sizes above in the same manner as you would assign prints. (Read manual for more details)

☐ Large at 800px for $ 15.00

☐ Medium at 600px for $ 10.00

☐ Small at 400px for $ 5.00

CANCEL   SAVE

The latest photo will appear first in a) its category and b) the Newest Photos section.

When a viewer passes the cursor over the thumbnail, a larger image will hover over the thumbnail. When the thumbnail is clicked, the viewer is taken to a product details page, where a larger preview image can be displayed.

The Add To Cart button is in place, and once clicked by a customer who has created an account in your store, it will take him to PayPal to make the purchase.

After the purchase, the customer is returned to his account page, where he can download the photo.

 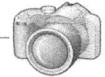

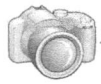

Other PhotoStore Features

▪ PhotoStore is compatible with other payment gateways, such as Authorize.net and 2Checkout.

▪ PhotoStore also accommodates shipping, in case you want to sell prints of your work.

▪ PhotoStore makes it possible to sell the work of other photographers. They can set up their own account and upload their photos for sale in your store. PhotoStore will keep track of all orders.

▪ PhotoStore gives you the option of offering subscriptions on a yearly or monthly basis. Subscribers get unlimited downloads during the subscription period.

ShopperPress

Setting up ShopperPress involves more effort than PhotoStore, but the lower price makes it worth it for some. And once you finish adding the first product, you will find it easy enough to work with.

After purchasing your copy of the ShopperPress WordPress theme, you need to download the theme, instruction manual, and license key. Online instructions will then tell you where to enter the license key within your account at Shopper Press.

Before beginning the setup, have the following options available:

1. WordPress 3.0 or higher installed.
2. ShopperPress 4.0 or higher installed.
3. FTP Access.

ShopperPress, a WordPress theme, needs to be uploaded into the "themes" folder:

wp-content/themes/

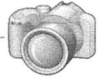

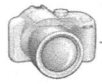
Next, upload the folder labeled "shopperpress." The directory structure will now read: wp-content/themes/shopperpress.

After uploading the theme, you need to activate it.

- Log in to your WordPress admin panel.

- In the left column, select Wordpress Appearance/Themes.

- Beneath the ShopperPress thumbnail, click on Activate.

- After activating the theme you will see a navigation menu for ShopperPress in the left column.

In this guide, we will use most of the default settings and designs. The following steps lay out the basic setup of ShopperPress using the PhotoShopper template design.

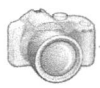

Step One

Choosing the Right Shopping Cart Type

For this guide, we will create a shopping cart site where users can purchase digital items, pay for them as normal at checkout, and download their product.

In the left column, under the ShopperPress heading, select General Setup. From the navigation tabs across the top, select System Setup. Then select Shopping Cart from the dropdown menu.

Underneath that section is another entitled Website Design. This area allows you to select a design theme for your store. Select PhotoShopper.

Next select your language and enter your copyright information.

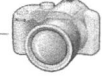

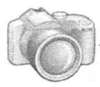

Step Two

Setting up Product Images

You will need to define the location for your image files. ShopperPress supports options for both locally hosted images and remotely hosted images.

Locally hosted images are those stored on your own hosting account; remotely hosted images are hosted elsewhere and you link to them.

We will be hosting the images locally, so we define the location by navigating to General Setup/Image Setup.

Image Caching should be enabled.

Under the heading Image Storage Folder (link), we will choose the default "thumbs" folder in ShopperPress. The path should look something like this:

http://www.yourdomain.com/wp-content/themes/shopperpress/thumbs/

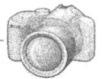

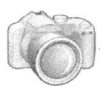

Under the heading Image Storage Folder (path), the path should look something like this:

/home/your_account/public_html/mediadesignphotography .com/wp-content/themes/shopperpress/thumbs/

The Image Storage fields will be filled in by default. Just check to be certain they are correct.

It's critical that file paths and links work correctly because this is where the system will try and grab the files for your customers to download after purchasing.

Note: The thumbs folder has a caching system. To display the images properly, you will need to CHMOD 777 the folder within the thumbs folder called "cache." Both the thumbs folder and cache folder should be CHMOD 777 for image management and display.

CHMOD 777 folders:

wp-content/themes/shopperpress/thumbs/
wp-content/themes/shopperpress/thumbs/cache/

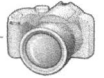

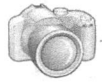

Step Three

Set up Checkout, Callback, and Contact Pages

ShopperPress has a number of built-in page templates that are used for the Checkout, Callback, Account, Profile, My Account, and My Profile pages. These are custom-built templates for ShopperPress.

You need to create these pages in WordPress and then assign the ShopperPress templates to each page. The User Manual contains a list of the pages that need to be created and associated with a template.

- In the left column, select Pages/New.

- Title the new page "Callback."

- In the right column, find the area labeled Template. From the dropdown menu, select the template that corresponds with the new page you've created.

- Repeat this process for each page.

Note: The User Manual contains a full listing of the pages that need to be created and associated with a template.

Step Four

Set Your Payment Gateways

▪ In the left column under ShopperPress, select Payment Setup.

▪ You should now see a list of payment gateways available with ShopperPress. Here, we will set up PayPal, so select PayPal gateway.

▪ Where you see Return URL, Cancel URL, and Notify URL, enter the link to the callback page you created earlier.

▪ The PayPal email is the one you already assigned to your PayPal account. The currency code should be USD or any of the correct currency codes set by PayPal.

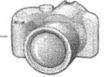

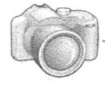
Step Five

Preparing Your Photos

I suggest you prepare your photos using Photoshop. Aiming to deliver the highest resolution available, we will open our photo in Photoshop and save it at the highest quality setting, with a label such as "vintage_cars1_master1.jpg".

- Now we create a copy of the master photo for the preview image. In the ShopperPress store, choose a width of 600 pixels and the default aspect ratio for height.

- Watermark the image by adding a layer. Use the text tool to add, say, your company name. Set the opaque to 50 percent.

- Save a copy of the preview image and assign it a label such as "vintage_cars1_lg1.jpg".

- Create a thumbnail image. Here we choose a width of 200 pixels and the default aspect ratio for height.

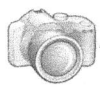

- Remove the layer that contains the watermark, save a copy of the thumbnail image, and assign it a label such as "vintage_cars1_th1.jpg".

- Zip up the master image for download after purchase. The zip file must have the same label as the master image file. Our master image is labeled "vintage_cars1_master1.jpg", so the zip file should be labeled "vintage_cars1_master1.zip".

- Finally, FTP the files over to your server. Upload them to the "thumbs" folder inside of the ShopperPress theme: wp-content/themes/shopperpress/thumbs/

Now you're ready to start adding your products to ShopperPress.

A watermark is a recognizable image or pattern that appears as various shades of lightness/darkness when viewed on a dark background. Watermarks are a great way to prevent unauthorized use of your photos.

 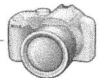

Screenshot #9

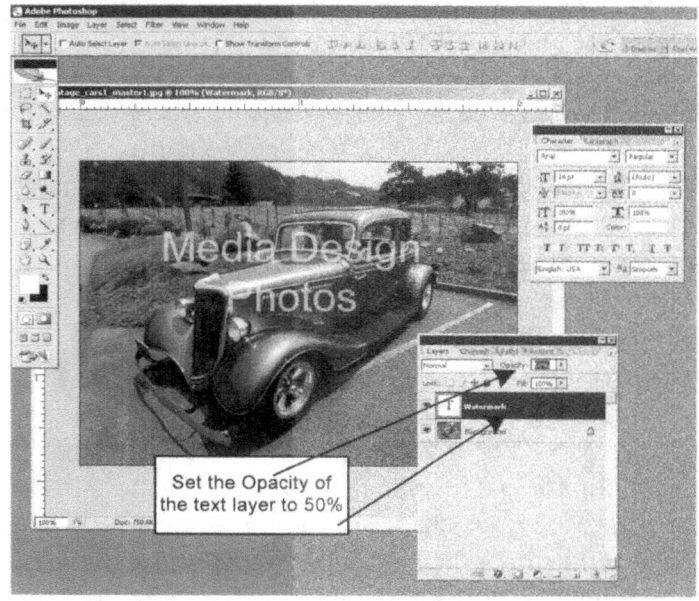

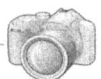

Step Six

Setting Up Your Products

First, you need to create your categories. In the left column under Posts, select Categories. Assign a title for the new category and click the button that says Add New Category.

Next, add your photos as products. In ShopperPress, products are added as new posts.

In the left column under Posts, select Add New. You will see various fields for defining product information, but we won't need most of those fields.

1. In the first field, assign a title for the new product.
2. In the right column, choose the category.
3. Under Item Type/Listing Type, use the default setting: Shop Product.
4. Under Product Details/Current Price, enter the price.
5. Under Quantity, enter a number value. Note: If you don't enter a number value here, the Add To Cart button will not appear next to the product.
6. Under Product Details/Filename, enter the name of the zip file that corresponds to the product file.

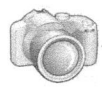
7. Under Image Details/Main Image, enter the URL of the thumbnail image. For example: http://www.mediadesignphotography.com/wp-content/themes/shopperpress/thumbs/seattle4_th4.jpg
8. Under Image Details/Gallery Images, enter the URL of the large preview image. Example: http://www.mediadesignphotography.com/wp-content/themes/shopperpress/thumbs/seattle4_lg4.jpg
9. In the Excerpt field, enter a brief description of your photo.
10. Click on the Update button in the upper-right column to publish your product.

You can view your newly added products by visiting your PhotoShopper webpage and clicking on the category. You will then see the thumbnails displayed.

Click on a thumbnail and you will be taken to the product description page. In the left column, you can preview the watermarked sample of the larger image by clicking on the thumbnail underneath the heading labeled View Large Image.

Screenshot #10

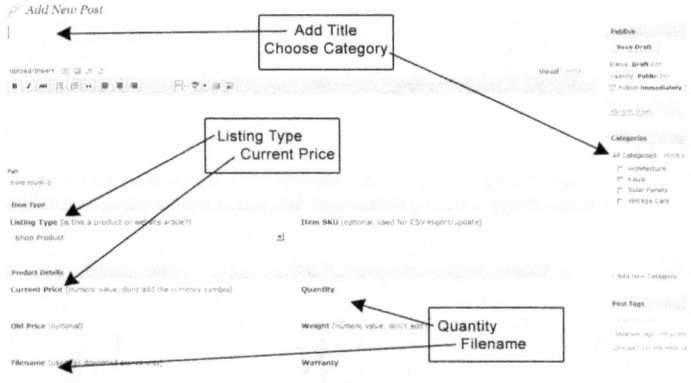

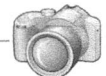

Screenshot #11

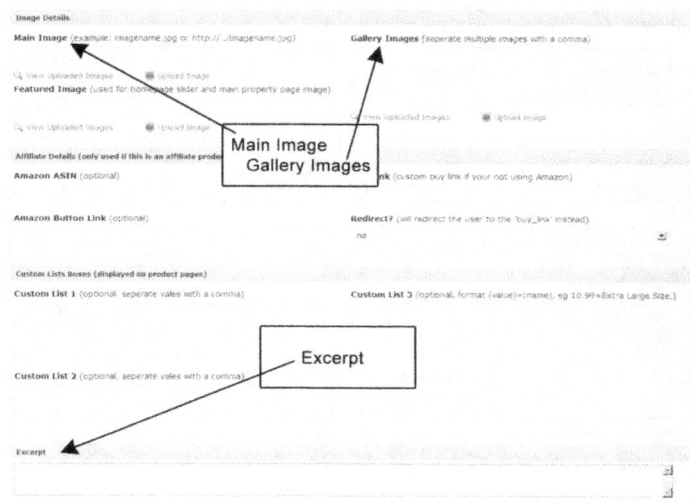

Screenshot #12

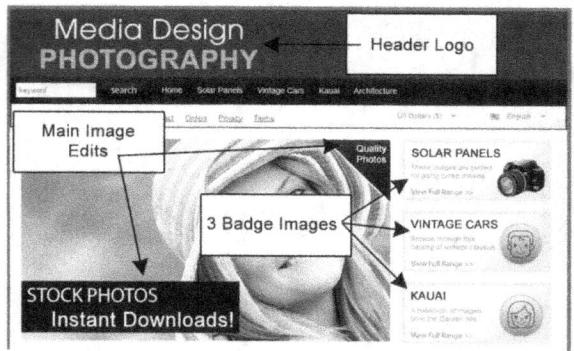

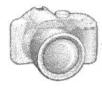

Step Seven

Modifying the Home Page

At some point you may want to modify some of the design elements of the Home Page in the PhotoShopper theme.

As you can see in Screenshot #12, I've chosen to modify the header logo, the large main image of the woman, and the three images to the right of that image.

You can locate the image files in the following folder:

shopperpress/themes/PhotoShopper/images

Header Logo

▪ In Photoshop, open the file labeled logo.png.

▪ Because the image size is 500 x 120, establish a Photoshop PSD file set to 500 x 120, with a transparent background.

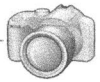

- Since the Photoshop file has a transparent background, we simply create a layer and use the text tool to add the name of our website.

- Add a new layer. Using the text tool, type in the name of your website. Save your file.

- Then save a png file and overwrite the original: File/Save for Web.

- Select PNG-24 to maintain the image quality and transparency.

- Assign the same filename as the original.

- Upload the new image to your server and overwrite the original.

Main Image

- In Photoshop, open the file labeled main.gif.

- The image size is 649 x 358, so set up a Photoshop PSD file at 649 x 358. Copy the original image and paste it into a new layer in your new PSD file.

- Use your color and text tools to create text that describes what type of products you are selling.

- Save your file.

- Save a gif file and overwrite the original: File/Save for Web.

- Select GIF and use the default settings. Assign the same filename as the original.

- Upload the new image to your server and overwrite the original.

Three Badge Images in the Right Column

- Open the file labeled badge2.gif in Photoshop.

- The image size is 251 x 98, so set up a Photoshop PSD file at 251 x 98. Copy the original image and paste it into a new layer in your new PSD file.

- Use your color and text tools to create text that defines the category to which the image will be linked.

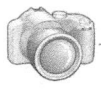
- Save your file.

- Save a gif file and overwrite the original: File/Save for Web.

- Select GIF and use the default settings. Assign the same filename as the original.

- Upload the new image to your server and overwrite the original.

- Repeat this process for the other two images: badge3.gif and badge4.gif.

Next we want to link these three images to the appropriate category pages.

- Go to the WordPress admin panel.

- In the left column, select ShopperPress/General Setup.

- Scroll down and find the section entitled Right Image Box 1.

- In the second field, insert the URL to the category
For example:
http://www.mediadesignphotography.com/category/solar
-panels/.

- Repeat this process for both Right Image Box 2 and
Right Image Box 3.

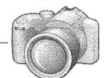

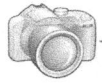

Other ShopperPress Benefits

ShopperPress has other settings you can adjust, including:

1. General Setup
2. Display Settings
3. Checkout
4. Shipping
5. Order History
6. Advertising
7. Analytics
8. Import Data
9. Payment Setup
10. Image Manager
11. Tools

The ShopperPress user manual is easy to follow. And although the program is sophisticated, it's simple in its approach to selling digital products via WordPress and PayPal.

If you're a photographer on a limited budget, ShopperPress offers an affordable way of getting your digital-photography store up and running.

ShopperPress also supports affiliate product sales for Amazon and Datafeedr.

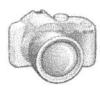
WordPress eStore Plugin

WordPress eStore is probably the most difficult of the three stores to set up. On the other hand, it is the least expensive of the three, and once you get a feel for adding products it's fairly easy to work with.

After you've downloaded the plugin, upload the folder "wp-cart-for-digital-products" to the /wp-content/plugins/ directory.

Activate the plugin as usual from the Plugins menu located in the left column in the WordPress admin panel.

Next, edit the settings. This can be done from the left column under WP eStore/Settings. Here you will edit commonplace items such as language, currency, and products per page. Everything in this area is self-explanatory.

Now create your categories. In the left column under WP eStore/Categories, enter the category name and click the Save Category button.

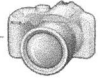

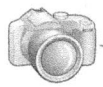

Adding Photos

Now you're ready to start adding your photos. In this case we will use the same photos we prepared in the previous ShopperPress chapter. The only difference: We won't use the thumbnail images. WordPress eStore will automatically resize the larger preview image into a thumbnail that, when clicked, will display a larger preview image.

We need to set up a folder in which to store the images, as well as the zipped-up images that will be downloaded after purchase.

- In the root area of your website, create a new folder and label it "downloads."

- Our sample site is www.mediadesignphotos.com, so our URL will look like this:
http://www.mediadesignphotos.com/downloads/

- Upload all of your display images and the zip files for product downloads.

▪ Return to the WordPress admin panel. Under the WP eStore section in the left column, select Add/Edit Products.

▪ Enter the product name and product price.

▪ Under Optional Product Details, drop down the section titled Additional Product Details.

▪ Enter a brief description of the photo in the Product Description field.

▪ In the field labeled Thumbnail Image URL, enter the full URL to the image inside the downloads folder.

Example:
http://www.mediadesignphotos.com/downloads/vintage_cars1_lg1.jpg

▪ Under Product Category, select the category from the dropdown menu.

▪ Drop down the section titled Digital Content Details.

▪ In the field labeled Digital Product URL, enter the full URL to the corresponding zip file inside the downloads folder.

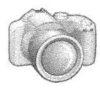

Example:
http://www.mediadesignphotos.com/downloads/vintage_cars1_master
1.zip

- Go to the bottom of the page and click on the Save Product button.

- Repeat this process for each of your image products.

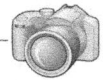

Screenshot #13

Add/Edit Products

You can add a new product or edit an existing product from this interface. When creating a new product you can choose to copy the details from an existing product too
when creating multiple products with similar details.

Product Details (Not sure how to add a product? Watch the video tutorial)

Product Name ◄——————————————————————————————————→ **Product Name**

      Name of the Product

Product Price ◄——————————————————————————————————→ **Product Price**

      Enter Price to two decimal places. Examples: 10.50 or 6.70 or 1999.95 etc (Do not put

Optional Product Details (If any of the following options is not needed for your product you can leave the field empty)

○ Additional Product Details (Click to Expand) ————————————————→ **Product Description**

Product Description ◄

      This description is used when displaying products using the fancy display option.

Thumbnail Image URL ◄——————————————————————————→ **Thumbnail Image URL**

      This thumbnail image is used when displaying products using the fancy display option.

Thumbnail Image Link ————————————————————————————→ **Product Category**

      If you want to link the thumbnail image to a URL then specify the target URL here otherwise leave empty.

Product Page URL

      If you have a specific page for detailed description of this product then specify the URL here otherwise leave empty. The product name will be linked to this

Product Category ◄   Select a Category ▼

Button Image URL

      This is useful when you want to use a custom button image than the one specified in the Settings menu for this product.

Button Link

      Only use this if you want the Add to Cart button for this product to go to the specified URL (eg. a landing page) instead of adding the product to the shopping
      product of others.

Display Quantity Field   ☐

      When checked, it will display a text box next to the Add to Cart button so the customer can enter a quantity amount for the item.

Collect Customer Input   ☐ Field Label

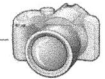

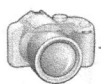

Screenshot #14

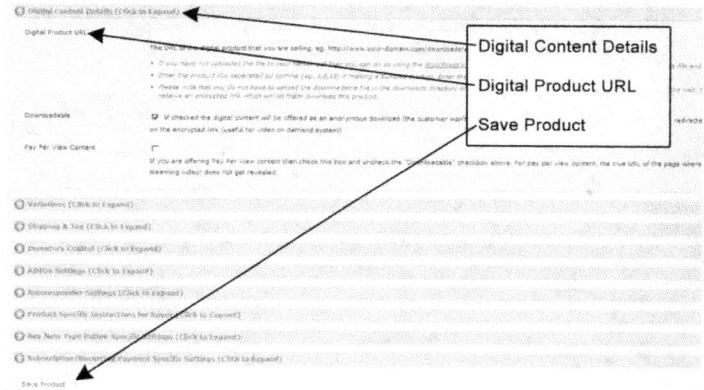

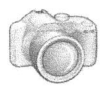

Setting up Product Posts

Now we will apply the product categories to WordPress Category and Posts.

▪ Create a category to correspond to each of the categories you set up in WP eStore.

▪ In the left column, select Posts/Categories. Under Add New Category, type in the name of the category and click on the Add New Category button.

▪ Next you will need to create a post for the products that you set up in WP eStore. In the left column, select Posts/Add New.

▪ Type in the Title.

▪ Switch the Text Editor over to HTML mode. WP eStore makes use of short codes, small pieces of HTML code that call a function from the plugin

▪ WP eStore has many different codes that you can implement in your store. You can download a complete list at the following address:

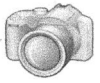

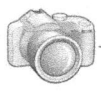

http://www.tipsandtricks-hq.com/ecommerce/wp-content/uploads/wp-estore-shortcodes.pdf

- The short codes require an additional plugin. You can download the plugin at the following address:

http://www.tipsandtricks-hq.com/ecommerce/wp-estore-shortcodes-and-functions-reference-460

After you download the plugin, it's time to upload the folder "eStore-extra-shortcodes" to the /wp-content/plugins/ directory. Activate the plugin as usual through the Plugins menu located in the left column in the WordPress admin panel.

- Now we insert a piece of code that will display all of the products for a particular category.

- After downloading the PDF file, you can copy and paste the following code:

[wp_eStore_category_products:category_id:4:end]

- You will need to replace category_id:4 with the category ID number that was assigned to the category when you set it up in WP eStore. You can find this number by going to the WP eStore menu in the left column and selecting Categories. You will see the category number listed to the left of each category you created.

- Next select a WordPress category from the right column and click on the Publish button. You now have a WordPress category that includes a post containing all the products you added to the WP eStore category. The post also contains an Add To Cart button.

- Finally, add the WP eStore Shopping Cart widget. WordPress widgets make calls to add-ons, such as search fields and navigational items that can be rearranged in the sidebar without editing PHP or HTML code. In the left column, select Appearance/Widgets.

- Locate the Widget labeled WP Cart for Digital Products and drag it onto the sidebar located on the right side.

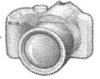

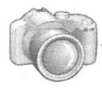

Note: The same setup applies whether you choose to display your products on individual pages or as individual posts.

You now have a WordPress store that contains posts with the image thumbnail, a preview of the larger image when the thumbnail is clicked, a description of the image, an Add To Cart button, a Shopping Cart display that shows the total items in cart, and a PayPal button to handle transactions and allow customers to download products.

You can view my sample site, Media Design Photos, at the following address:

http://www.mediadesignphotos.com

Note: Although WordPress eStore Plugin does not offer much of a user manual, there is plenty of online documentation and support. And if you're on a limited budget, you'll appreciate the $39.95 price tag.

Screenshot #15

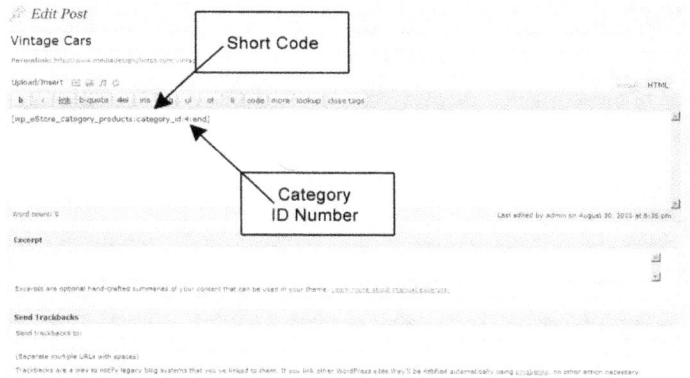

 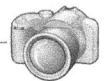

Promoting Your New Online Store

I now offer my favorite techniques for promoting sites and developing pagerank. When using WordPress, I often find my new sites spidered and indexed in Google within twenty-four hours. This is largely due to the pinging services that WordPress notifies.

Pinging

Update services—Pings—are tools that let other people know you've updated your blog. WordPress automatically notifies popular Update Services, such as Ping-o-Matic, that you've made such an update by sending a ping each time you create or modify a post. In turn, update services process the ping and edit their databases with your site's update. The title of your new content and an excerpt will appear in the update, along with a link back to the post's web address.

Ping lists can be added from your WordPress dashboard. In the left navigation column, select Settings/Writing. At the bottom of the Writing page, look for a field labeled Update Services. Paste in your list of ping services, and click on the button labeled Save Changes.

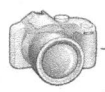

You can obtain a comprehensive Ping list at:
www.prelovac.com/vladimir/wordpress-ping-list.

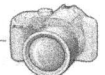

RSS Feeds

Another great feature of WordPress is that it produces RSS (Real Simple Syndication) feeds of the content on your site. There are hundreds of RSS feed directories, and other websites will pull the feeds from those directories and display the feed content on their own sites. The feeds contain a link back to the source of the feed, thus providing you with potential traffic and another backlink to your site.

I use a program called Traffic Mania RSS Bot, which submits our feeds to about 40 RSS feed directories. You can find out more about RSS Bot at www.incansoft.com.

It will help the online promotion of your new site if you build backlinks on a regular basis; however, if you find that you are building backlinks haphazardly, or not at all, consider outsourcing your SEO campaign to a certified SEO consultant.

More tips on backlinking and promoting your site can be found at Basic SEO Direct, www.basicseodirect.com.

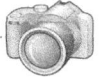

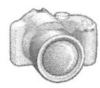

Press Releases

Many people don't appreciate the value of press releases, but it's a method I regularly use for promoting my sites. You can pay as much as $100 for a press release at PRWeb, or you can submit to the many free press-release sites.

To submit to free press-release sites, I use a program called Traffic Mania Press Bot. It provides a template for compiling your press release so that it conforms to standard press-release protocol.

You can find more information about Press Bot here:

http://www.incansoft.com

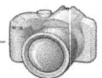

Backlinking

In addition to Pings, you will want to obtain backlinks from other sites, for indexing purposes and to improve pagerank. Here are two suggestions for effective backlinking:

1. If you have any preexisting sites, or know people who have sites that have age, pagerank, or are regularly spidered by the search engines, add a link to your new site.

2. I have a subscription with USFreeads (www.usfreeads.com), and once I set up a new site, I place a classified ad there that contains a link back to the new site. My ad contains only the title of the site, a description, a price tag of zero, and the web address. Google spiders USFreeads every hour, so you will see your ad indexed in Google immediately. The Google spider will then follow the link to your site.

 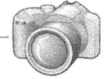

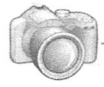

Adwords

Another way to promote your new online store is to make use of Google Adwords. AdWords is Google's flagship advertising product and main source of revenue. AdWords offers pay-per-click (PPC) advertising for both text and banner ads. Google's text advertisements are short, consisting of one title line and two content text lines.

Adwords can be pricey because advertisers bid for ad placement. If your site's niche is highly competitive—say, weight loss or cosmetic surgery—you may want to avoid this approach. On the other hand, if you face little competition, you may be able to purchase advertising for as little as five cents per click.

Make sure the ad's "click thru" URL points to your new photography store.

You can learn more about creating an Adwords account and implementing your advertising campaign by visiting Adwords at http://adwords.google.com.

Social Bookmarking Sites

I find backlinking through social bookmarking sites to be a powerful method for obtaining high pagerank and search positioning. Social bookmarking is a way for Internet users to share, organize, search, and manage bookmarks of web resources. Unlike file sharing, the resources themselves aren't shared, merely bookmarks that reference them.

Social bookmarking helps search engines find and rank content through links. Backlinking through these sites will help promote traffic to your site, contribute to your link-building campaign, and increase your search-engine rankings.

It may be worth your while to spend a few dollars and obtain thousands of legitimate backlinks. We use a company that provides backlinking through a network of over 350 social bookmarking sites spread over four continents. The process requires submitting your site's RSS feeds to the bookmarking sites. This is yet another benefit of using WordPress, which automatically generates RSS feeds and updates them every time you add new content.

You can find out more about backlinking to social book-marking sites at Basic SEO Direct, www.basicseodirect.com.

Summary

Over the years, I've come to realize that most photographers are technically challenged when it comes to promoting their portfolio of work online. Many are simply too busy to establish a web presence using sophisticated methods and design programs.

In this book I've detailed three different approaches to establishing that presence without having to depend on outside developers. I've outlined the setup procedures, suggested popular search-engine-optimization techniques, and offered ways to promote your new online presence.

For some photographers, setting up an online photography store will become a vital tool for selling and promoting their work online. For others, it just may be a way to earn additional income and have fun sharing their work with others.

If you're on a limited budget, or just want to dabble in digital photo sales, the two inexpensive approaches I outlined may be the best route.

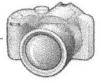

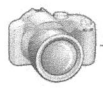

But if you want to take a shot at making extra money online, the PhotoStore option is definitely worth considering, especially given its built-in feature for selling the work of other photographers.

I hope this book provides you with the tools and insights necessary to develop a web presence for your online photography store.

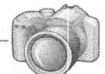

Professional Development Services

Too busy to set up your online store?

Media Design Services, Inc. is a web and multimedia company specializing in website development, Internet marketing, and online shopping. Media Design Services developed all the stores included in this book. For more information regarding customized web services, contact Media Design Services.

Media Design Services, Inc.
P.O. Box 3153
Santa Rosa, CA 95402
707-836-8389

Email: blake@mediadesign-mds.com

Expression Web and Dreamweaver Templates
http://www.templatemill.com

Flash Templates
http://www.flashdesigntemplates.com

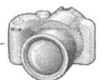

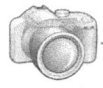

Stock Photography
http://www.mediastockphotos.com

Search Engine Optimization
http://www.basicseodirect.com

Glossary

AdSense

An ad-serving application run by Google. Website owners can enroll in this program to enable text, image, and video advertisements on their websites.

Affiliate

The publisher/salesperson in an affiliate marketing relationship.

Affiliate Marketing

An Internet-based marketing practice in which a business rewards one or more affiliates for each visitor or customer generated by the affiliate's marketing efforts.

 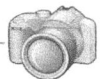

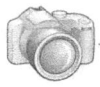

Application Programming Interface (API)

An interface implemented by a software program to enable interaction with other software, much as a user-interface facilitates interaction between humans and computers.

Cookie

A message from a web-server computer, sent to and stored by your browser on your computer. When your computer consults the originating server computer, the cookie is sent back to the server, allowing it to respond to you according to the cookie's contents. Cookies are mainly used to provide customized webpages based on a profile of your interests.

cPanel

cPanel is a Unix-based web-hosting control panel that provides a graphical interface and automation tools designed to simplify the process of hosting a website.

 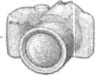

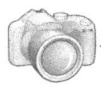

Digital Camera

A digital camera (also digicam or camera for short) is a camera that digitally takes video or still photographs, or both, by recording images via an electronic image sensor.

Digital Photography

Digital photography is a form of photography that uses digital technology to make images of subjects. Digital photographs can be displayed, printed, stored, manipulated, transmitted, and archived using digital and computer techniques, without chemical processing.

Dofollow

This is provided in the HTML page of a website in order to direct search engines to follow that particular link to another webpage or site.

Dreamweaver

Popular web-development and editing software. Developed by Adobe.

FrontPage

Web-development software for the Windows platform. Developed by Microsoft.

FTP (File Transfer Protocol)

One of the most common methods for sending files between two computers.

FTP Server

A web server you can log on to, download files from, and upload files to. Anonymous FTP is a method for downloading files from an FTP server without using a log-on account.

HTML (Hypertext Markup Language)

HTML, the language of the web, is a set of tags that define the content, layout, and formatting of the web document. Web browsers use HTML tags to define the display of the text.

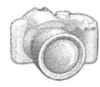

Keyword

In web terms: A word used by a search engine to search for relevant web information.

In database terms: A word (or index) used to identify a database record.

Meta Description

A description tag intended as a brief summary of a webpage's content.

Meta Keyword

A tag used to spotlight the keywords used in a webpage.

MySQL

Free open-source database software often used on the web.

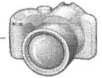

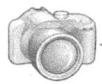

Name Server

In computing, a name server (also nameserver) consists of a program or computer server that implements a name-service protocol. It maps a human-recognizable identifier to a system-internal, often numeric, identification or addressing component.

Niche

A niche market is the subset of the market on which a specific product is focused. The market niche defines the specific product features aimed at satisfying specific market needs, as well as the price range, production quality, and demographics it is intended to impact.

Nofollow

Nofollow provides a way for webmasters to tell search engines, "Don't follow links on this page" or "Don't follow this specific link."

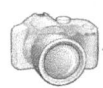

Online Shopping

Online shopping is the process whereby consumers directly buy goods or services from a seller in real time, without an intermediary service, over the Internet.

Parameter

An item of information, such as a name, number, or selected option, that is passed to a program by a user or another program.

Plugin

An application built into another application.

RSS Feed

RSS (Really Simple Syndication) is a family of web-feed formats used to publish frequently updated works—such as blog entries, news headlines, audio, and video—in a standardized format.

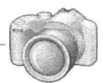

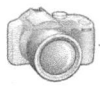

Search Engine

Computer program used to search and catalog (index) the millions of pages of available information on the web. Common search engines are Google, Yahoo, and Bing.

Search Engine Optimization (SEO)

The process of improving the volume or quality of traffic to a website from search engines via "natural" or unpaid (also: "organic" or "algorithmic") search results; as opposed to search engine marketing (SEM), which deals with paid inclusion.

Spam

The action of sending multiple unwelcome email messages to a newsgroup or mailing list.

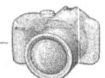

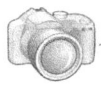

Spider

A computer program that searches the Internet for webpages. Web spiders include the ones used by search engines like Google and Yahoo to index the web. Spiders are also called robots.

URL (Uniform Resource Locator)

A web address. The standard way to address webpages on the Internet. For example: http://www.yahoo.com.

WordPress

WordPress is an open source CMS, often used as a blog-publishing application powered by PHP and MySQL. It has many features, including a plugin architecture and a templating system. WordPress is the most popular blog software in use today.

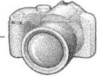

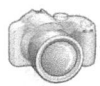

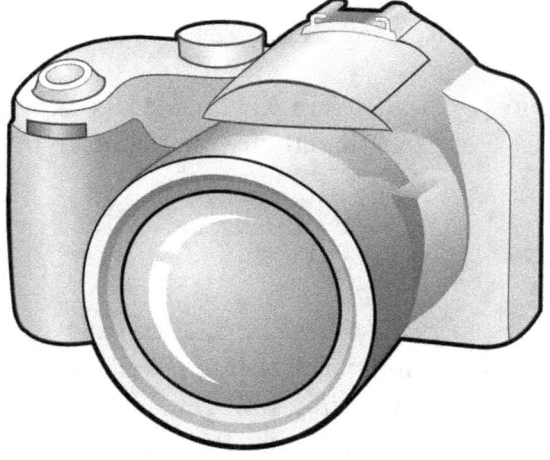

 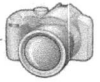

www.ingramcontent.com/pod-product-compliance
Lightning Source LLC
Chambersburg PA
CBHW060147200526
45165CB00023B/969

* 9 7 8 1 4 5 3 8 6 4 0 7 4 *